WALKABOUT
Flowers

Editor: **Ambreen Husain**
Design: **Volume One**

Photographs: Heather Angel—13, 18, 26; Bruce
Coleman Ltd.—(E. Crichton) 7 inset, 11, 14, 15,
(J. Grayson) 9, (J. Cowan) 21, (C. Wallace) 22-23,
(K. Taylor) 27, (P. Ward) 28, (J. Burton) 29,
(D. Orchard) 30; DLP Photo Library—(David
Heald) 8; Eye Ubiquitous—(P. Claydon) 16,
(J. Northover) 17, (K. Oldroyd) 24, cover; Chris
Fairclough Colour Library—5, 6, 25; NHPA—
(L. Campbell) 12; Oxford Scientific Films—
(H. Fox) 10, (S. Osolinski) 19; Photos
Horticultural—7; Kenneth Scowen—20, 31.

Library of Congress Cataloging-in-Publication Data

Pluckrose, Henry Arthur.
   Flowers / by Henry Pluckrose.
      p. cm. — (Walkabout)
   ISBN 0-516-08117-9
      1. Flowers—Miscellanea—Juvenile literature.
   2. Plants—Miscellanea—Juvenile literature.
   [1. Flowers. 2. Plants.] I. Title. II. Series:
   Pluckrose, Henry Arthur. Walkabout.
   QK49.P54   1994
   582.13—dc20   93-45661
                                                   CIP
                                                   AC

1994 Childrens Press® Edition
© 1993 Watts Books, London
1 2 3 4 5 6 7 8 9 0 R 03 02 01 00 99 98 97 96 95 94

WALKABOUT
Flowers

Henry Pluckrose

CHILDRENS PRESS ®

CHICAGO

Flowers seem to grow
almost everywhere.
These woodland
flowers are
wildflowers.
They grow wherever
there is warmth,
sunlight, water,
and soil.

Garden flowers grow
where we plant them.
They also need
warmth, sunlight,
water, and soil.

Flowers grow from
seeds, bulbs, or stems
called corms.
If we plant these seeds
in spring, they will
grow into flowering
plants by summer.

6

If we plant these bulbs in the fall, they will grow into spring flowers.

Plants have roots that push down into the soil. The roots find the water and the chemicals that the plant needs in the soil.

The leaves of a plant contain a green pigment called chlorophyll.
The leaves use chlorophyll and sunlight to make food. They turn the water and chemicals carried by the roots into sugar.
Sugar is the food that the plant needs to live.

There are many kinds
of flowers.
Each kind of flower has its
own special shape.
The petals on this pansy are
round and flat.

Some flowers, like these lilies, look like a trumpet.

Others are umbrella-shaped

or round like a ball,

narrow and pointed,

or simply spiky!

There are flowering plants
called bushes

and flowering plants
that climb.

There are flowers that
grow in water

and flowers that grow
in hot, dry places.

There are flowers
that grow on trees

and flowers that
grow in walls.

There are flowers
in many colors and
flowers of many sizes.

But why do plants
have flowers?

23

Each flower head
contains new life . . .
seeds for next
year's plants.
In order to grow,
seeds must be fertilized
with pollen from another plant
of the same kind.

Every flower contains nectar
—a sweet-smelling liquid.
Bees, butterflies, and other
insects collect the nectar
from inside the flower.

As a bee moves down
inside the flower to
drink the nectar,
pollen from the flower
sticks onto its legs.

The bee carries this pollen
with it from plant to plant . . .
and fertilizes the seeds.
Can you see the yellow pollen?

When the flower dies,
the seeds that have
been fertilized
begin to grow and ripen.
This is the seed case
of a poppy.

Where there was once
a dandelion flower,
there is now
a head of tiny seeds.

29

We grow flowers in parks
and gardens, in pots
and in window boxes . . .
and even in huge fields.

Index

About this book

Young children acquire information in a casual, almost random fashion. Indeed, they learn just by being alive! The books in this series complement the way young children learn. Through photographs and a simple text the readers are encouraged to comment on the world around them.

To a young child, the world is new and almost everything in it is interesting. But interest alone is not enough. If a child is to grow intellectually this interest has to be directed and extended. This book uses a well-tried and successful method of achieving this goal. By focusing on a particular topic, it invites the reader first to look and then to question. The words and photographs provide a starting point for discussion.

Children enjoy information books just as much as stories and poetry. For those who are not yet able to read print, this book provides pictures that encourage talk and visual discrimination—a vital part of the learning process.

Henry Pluckrose